STARS OF SPORTS

KEVIN
DURANT

BASKETBALL CHAMPION

■■■ by Matt Chandler

CAPSTONE PRESS
a capstone imprint

Stars of Sports is published by Capstone Press, an imprint of Capstone
1710 Roe Crest Drive, North Mankato, Minnesota 56003
www.capstonepub.com

**Library of Congress Cataloging-in-Publication Data is available on the Library
of Congress website.**
ISBN: 978-1-5435-9170-5 (library binding)
ISBN: 978-1-5435-9184-2 (ebook PDF)

Summary: Standing over 6 feet tall while in middle school, Kevin Durant seemed
destined for basketball greatness. He was heavily recruited after high school and
never folded under the pressure. From NBA Rookie of the Year to the NBA finals
MVP, Durant has proven himself time and time again.

Editorial Credits
Christianne Jones, editor; Ashlee Suker, designer; Eric Gohl, media researcher;
Laura Manthe, production specialist

Image Credits
Associated Press: Eric Gay, 6; Newscom: ABACAUSA.COM/David Santiago, 21,
Cal Sport Media/John Green, 11, Icon SMI/AJ Mast , 9, Icon SMI/Brian Ray, 12,
Icon SMI/Larry Smith, 13, Reuters/Anthony Bolante, 19, Reuters/Mike Segar, 15,
20, Reuters/Shannon Stapleton, 17, TNS/Jose Carlos Fajardo, 22, USA Today Sports/
Brian Spurlock, 23, USA Today Sports/Ken Blaze, cover, USA Today Sports/Kyle
Terada, 5, 25, 28; Shutterstock: A.RICARDO, 27, EFKS, 1

All internet sites appearing in back matter were available and accurate when this
book was sent to press.

Printed in the United States of America.
PA99

TABLE OF CONTENTS

Glossary terms are **BOLD** on first use.

There were five minutes left in game five of the 2017 NBA Finals. Golden State Warriors superstar Kevin Durant drove to the basket. His **layup** gave the Warriors a 12-point lead over the Cleveland Cavaliers.

The Warriors were up 3-1 in the series. Durant was set on winning the final game at home. He had had a monster series. He led his team in scoring in all five games. But he saved his best for game five.

Durant scored 39 points. As the clock ticked down to zero, Durant dribbled the ball up the court. The buzzer sounded. The Warriors won! "KD," as he is known, had led his team to the 2017 NBA Title!

Kevin Durant adds to the Warriors lead with a slam dunk. 〉〉〉

CHAPTER ONE

BORN TO BALL

Kevin Durant was born in Seat Pleasant, Maryland, in 1988. He had a hard childhood. He was one of four children. His father left the family before Durant turned one. He was raised by his mother and grandmother. They didn't have much money.

All around him, Durant saw people struggle. The community was poor. There were drugs and fighting. Because of this, the family had to move a lot. He went to seven different schools. It wasn't easy to make friends.

Kevin Durant knew he had to get out as soon as he could. And he knew basketball was the only way he would get out.

‹‹‹ Durant celebrates a big win with his mom.

GOAL SETTER

When he was around 10 years old, Durant told his mom he wanted to play in the NBA. It was a big goal. The odds were against him. But Durant didn't want to be poor anymore. He wanted to help his family. So he practiced and practiced and practiced.

Durant went to three different high schools. During that time, he grew 7 inches. He was 6 feet 9 inches tall by his senior year. Durant was one of the top high school basketball players in the country. College coaches took notice.

FACT

Durant was so tall and talented as a youth basketball player, his travel team had to carry a copy of his birth certificate to games to prove he wasn't too old!

〉〉〉 In 2005, Durant attended the Nike
All-American basketball camp.

Not many young men who grew up where
Durant did ever made it to college. But Durant
was determined to get out and have a better life.
In 2006, he accepted a **scholarship** to play at the
University of Texas.

CHAPTER TWO

TEXAS LONGHORN

Durant had the talent to go from high school to the NBA. In 2006, he was named a McDonald's All-American. The honor is given to the best high school basketball players in the country. Durant was named MVP of the 2006 McDonald's All-American game.

Durant had enough talent to skip college and turn pro. But one year before Durant finished high school, the NBA changed the rules. A player now had to be one year out of high school before they could play in the NBA.

Pro ball would have to wait. Instead, Kevin Durant would attend college at the University of Texas. He got a full basketball scholarship. Durant was going to be a Longhorn.

Durant at the McDonald's All-American game in 2006. 〉〉〉

FRESHMAN SUPERSTAR

Durant proved himself right away. He started every game during his freshman year. He averaged almost 26 points and more than 11 **rebounds** per game.

Durant showed he was ready for the NBA when his team played **rival** Texas Tech on January 31, 2007. He took over the game, scoring 37 points. The big man added 23 rebounds. Tech had no answer for Durant.

Durant as a college freshman. 〉〉〉

>>> Durant grabs a rebound against Oklahoma.

With the game well in hand, Durant added some extra excitement. The Longhorns were moving down the court. Guard D.J. Augustin was headed for an easy **layup**. Instead, he tossed an underhanded **alley-oop** to Durant. Durant soared high and slammed the ball down into the net.

CHAPTER THREE

ONE AND DONE

Durant lead the Texas Longhorns to the NCAA tournament in 2007. He also won the Naismith Trophy. This award goes to the best college basketball player. Durant was the first freshman to ever win the respected award.

Now Durant had a decision to make. He could continue his education and college basketball career, or he could go pro. If he stayed in college, he would risk getting hurt. Durant thought it was the right time for him to take the next step.

Kevin Durant knew he wanted to play in the NBA. And he knew he was ready. He was not going to wait any longer. Durant was going to make his childhood dream come true.

〉〉〉 Durant at the 2007 NBA **Draft** in New York City.

FACT

Durant became a multimillionaire before he ever stepped onto an NBA court. Nike signed the 18-year-old to a $60 million deal in the summer of 2007.

DRAFT DAY

Durant had spent thousands of hours of practicing. He had played basketball at three different high schools. He left home in Maryland to play college basketball in Texas. He had a dream. And on June 28, 2007, that dream came true.

"With the second pick in the 2007 NBA Draft, the Seattle SuperSonics select Kevin Durant, from the University of Texas."

With those words from NBA Commissioner David Stern, Durant's professional career began. Durant was just 18 years old. One year earlier he was a high school student. Now he was a professional basketball player!

Durant rose from his seat and hugged his mom. He joined Stern on the stage. He put on a Seattle SuperSonics hat and a huge smile.

After being drafted, Durant smiled and shook hands 〉〉〉 with NBA Commissioner David Stern.

Oden vs. Durant

Durant is one of the best players in the NBA today.
But in 2007, the Portland Trail Blazers skipped him
in the draft. They used the number one pick to select
center Greg Oden. It is considered by many experts to
be the biggest mistake in NBA draft history.

LIFE IN THE NBA

Many players struggle in their **rookie** season. The leap from college to the NBA is huge. The pressure to perform is too much for some players. Durant made it look easy.

His NBA career began in Denver on Halloween 2007. His SuperSonics took on the Denver Nuggets. Durant didn't look like he was nervous at all. He scored 18 points. He added three steals and five rebounds as well.

The SuperSonics lost their first eight games of the season. And they kept on losing. They finished the season with a terrible record of 20-62.

But Durant had amazing numbers. He averaged more than 20 points per game in 80 games. He added 348 rebounds, 75 blocked shots, and 78 steals. It all added up to Durant winning the NBA Rookie of the Year Award.

As a rookie, Durant was in the starting lineup for 80 of the Sonics 82 games.

OKLAHOMA SUPERSTAR

Following his rookie season, the SuperSonics left Seattle. They became the Oklahoma City Thunder. The move didn't slow down Durant. He led the Thunder in points and minutes per game. Along with teammate Russell Westbrook, Durant gave Thunder fans a reason to be excited for the future.

With Durant leading the way, the Thunder made the playoffs for the next six seasons. In 2012, he led the NBA in points per game. He carried the Thunder to the NBA Finals. They lost the series four games to one. But Durant became a true superstar.

⟩⟩⟩ Durant against LeBron James in game 5 of the 2012 NBA Finals.

Despite tight defense, Durant gets a shot off. 〉〉〉

FREE AGENCY

After nine seasons with the team that drafted him, Durant became a **free agent**. He had earned six All-Star selections. He led the league in scoring four times.

The Golden State Warriors won the NBA title in 2015. With stars Steph Curry, Klay Thomson, and Draymond Green, the Warriors were considered a top team. On July 7, 2016, Durant signed a two-year, $54 million **contract** to join the Warriors.

》》》 Teammates Draymond Green (second from right) and Stephen Curry (far right) congratulate Durant.

<<< Another epic dunk by Durant

Durant said he was making the best move for himself and his family. It was also a move that worked out very well for his new team.

Durant averaged 25.1 points per game in his first season at Golden State. That included a big performance against his former team. He led the Warriors with 39 points in a 122-96 win over the Thunder early in the season.

CHAPTER FIVE

MVP

In 2017, the Cleveland Cavaliers faced the Golden State Warriors in the NBA Finals. It was a rematch of the 2016 Finals. The Cavs were the champions and looking to repeat. Durant made sure that didn't happen. He put up 35 points per game in the finals. The Cavaliers were no match for Durant. The Warriors won the series 4-1.

Durant's value to the Warriors became even more obvious in the 2019 playoffs. He scored 45 or more points in three games. He shot 51 percent from three-point range. The Warriors looked like a lock to win their third straight NBA title.

Then Durant got hurt in game five of the Western Conference Semifinals. Without Durant, the Warriors were no match for the Toronto Raptors in the NBA Finals. They lost the series 4-2.

〉〉〉 Durant earned the NBA Finals MVP award in 2018.

Double MVP

In the 2017 Finals, Durant earned his first Finals MVP award. The following year the Warriors faced Cleveland in a rematch. Durant led the Warriors to a sweep of the Cavs and his second Finals MVP trophy!

NEXT STOP

In today's NBA, very few players stick with one team. Some chase the most money. Others chase a chance at a title. Durant has the money. He has the titles. He has the MVP awards. So where would Durant be playing ball next?

In the summer of 2019, Durant was linked to the New York Knicks. Other people expected Durant to finish his career with the Warriors.

On June 30, 2019, Durant shocked the basketball world. He announced that he would be signing with the Brooklyn Nets. On July 7, Durant made it official. He signed a four-year contract with the Brooklyn Nets for $164 million.

FACT

Durant is a two-time Olympic Gold Medalist. He won gold in the 2012 and 2016 Olympics as a member of Team USA.

KD'S LEGACY

How will Kevin Durant be remembered when his career is over? Durant proved he was a leader for the Warriors. The team won back-to-back titles with him. He earned MVP honors in both Finals.

There is little doubt Durant will earn a spot in the NBA Hall of Fame. Time will tell if he is seen as the greatest small forward to ever play the game.

〉〉〉 Durant posed with a few of his many trophies.

TIMELINE

1988   born on September 29 in Maryland

2006   attends the University of Texas; averages more than 25 points per game in his only season of college basketball

2007   joins the Seattle SuperSonics with the second overall pick in the NBA Draft

2012   wins first gold medal as part of the United States basketball team at the London Olympics

2014   earns the NBA's Most Valuable Player (MVP) title

2016   signs a two-year, $54 million deal with the Golden State Warriors

2017   leads team over the Cavaliers and is named MVP of the NBA Finals

2018   earns second straight Finals MVP Award as the Warriors sweep the Cavaliers

2019   makes tenth consecutive NBA All-Star team

2019   ruptures Achilles tendon in game five of the NBA Finals

2019   signs a 4-year deal with the Brooklyn Nets

GLOSSARY

ALLEY-OOP (al-ee-OOP)—high pass made toward the basket, so a teammate can catch the ball in the air and slam dunk it

CONTRACT (KAHN-trakt)—a legal agreement

DRAFT (DRAFT)—an event in which athletes are picked to join sports organizations or teams

FREE AGENT (FREE AY-juhnt)—a player who is free to sign with any team

LAYUP (LAY-uhp)—a close shot where the ball is gently played off the backboard and into the hoop

REBOUND (REE-bound)—the act of gaining possession of the ball after a missed shot

RIVAL (RYE-vuhl)—someone whom a person competes against

ROOKIE (RUK-ee)—a first-year player

SCHOLARSHIP (SKOL-ur-ship)—money given to a student to pay for school

READ MORE

Chandler, Matt. *Pro Basketball Records*. North Mankato, MN: Capstone Press, 2019.

Gitlin, Marty. *Kevin Durant*. Mendota Heights, MN: North Star Editions, 2017.

Nagelhout, Ryan. *20 Fun Facts About Basketball*. New York: Gareth Stevens, 2016.

INTERNET SITES

Jr. NBA
www.jr.nba.com

Online Basketball Drills
www.online-basketball-drills.com

USA Basketball
www.usab.com

INDEX